Children's Room
Rock Island Public Library
401 - 19th Street
Rock Island, IL 61201-8143

NOV - - 2014

D1289475

Superstars of the ST. LOUIS CARDINALS

by Annabelle Tometich

amicus
high interest

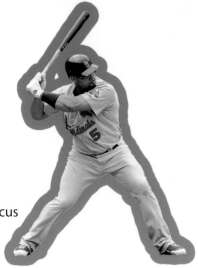

Amicus High Interest is published by Amicus
P.O. Box 1329, Mankato, MN 56002
www.amicuspublishing.us

Copyright © 2015. International copyright reserved in all countries.
No part of this book may be reproduced in any form without written
permission from the publisher.

Library of Congress Cataloging-in-Publication Data
Tometich, Annabelle, 1980-
  Superstars of the St. Louis Cardinals / by Annabelle Tometich.
     pages cm. -- (Pro sports superstars)
  Includes bibliographical references and index.
  Summary: "Presents some of the St. Louis Cardinals' greatest players and
their achievements in pro baseball, including Ozzie Smith, Albert Pujols,
and Yadier Molina"--Provided by publisher.
  ISBN 978-1-60753-597-3 (hardcover : alk. paper) -- ISBN 978-1-60753-630-
7 (pdf ebook)
  1. St. Louis Cardinals (Baseball team)--History--Juvenile literature.
2. Baseball players--United States--Juvenile literature. I. Title.
  GV875.S3T66 2014
  796.357'640977866--dc23
                        2013044092

Photo Credits: Jeff Roberson/AP Images, cover, 16; Aspen Photo/
Shutterstock Images, 2, 15; Matt Slocum/AP Images, 5; Bettmann/Corbis,
7, 13; AP Images, 8; Warren M. Winterbottom/AP Images, 10; Matt York/AP
Images, 19; Jared Wickerham/AP Images, 21, 22

Produced for Amicus by The Peterson Publishing Company
and Red Line Editorial.

Editor Arnold Ringstad
Designer Maggie Villaume
Printed in the United States of America
Mankato, MN
2-2014
PA10001
10 9 8 7 6 5 4 3 2 1

TABLE OF CONTENTS

MEET THE ST. LOUIS CARDINALS

The St. Louis Cardinals have won 11 **World Series**. The team is more than 100 years old. It has had many stars. Here are some of the best.

JAY HANNA "DIZZY" DEAN

Dizzy Dean was a pitcher. He helped the Cardinals win the 1934 World Series. He threw powerful **fastballs**. He entered the **Hall of Fame** in 1953.

The 1934 Cardinals were nicknamed "the Gashouse Gang."

8

ENOS SLAUGHTER

Enos Slaughter is famous for his Mad Dash. It happened in the 1946 World Series. The Cardinals played the Boston Red Sox. Slaughter ran from first base to home plate. He scored the winning run.

STAN MUSIAL

Stan Musial was a great hitter. His nickname was "Stan the Man." Musial started playing in 1941. He hit 475 **home runs**.

Musial was in the navy during World War II.

BOB GIBSON

Bob Gibson was a pitcher. He led the Cardinals to two World Series. Gibson's pitches were very fast. They were hard for batters to hit. He won an **MVP** award in 1968.

14

OZZIE SMITH

Ozzie Smith was a great **shortstop**. His nickname was the "Wizard of Oz." He was smart and quick on defense. He helped St. Louis win the 1982 World Series.

Smith sometimes did a backflip when he walked onto the field.

ALBERT PUJOLS

Albert Pujols played first base. He hit 445 home runs. Pujols helped the Cardinals win two World Series. The last one was in 2011.

17

YADIER MOLINA

Yadier Molina is a catcher. He has won six **Gold Glove Awards**. The first one came in 2008. He is good at throwing out runners.

MICHAEL WACHA

Michael Wacha is a young pitcher. His first game was in 2013. He quickly became a star.

The Cardinals have had many great superstars. Who will be next?

21

TEAM FAST FACTS

Founded: 1882

Other names: St. Louis Brown Stockings (1882), St. Louis Browns (1883–1898), St. Louis Perfectos (1899)

Nicknames: The Cards, the Redbirds, the Birds

Home Stadium: Busch Stadium (St. Louis, Missouri)

World Series Championships: 11 (1926, 1931, 1934, 1942, 1944, 1946, 1964, 1967, 1982, 2006, and 2011)

Hall of Fame Players: 38, including Dizzy Dean, Stan Musial, Enos Slaughter, Bob Gibson, and Ozzie Smith

WORDS TO KNOW

fastballs – pitches that go fast and straight

Gold Glove Awards – awards given to the best fielders each year

Hall of Fame – a group of baseball players voted the best ever

home runs – hits that go far enough to leave the field, letting the hitter run all the way around the bases to score a run

MVP – Most Valuable Player; an honor given to the best player each season

shortstop – a player whose main job is to stop balls hit between second and third base

World Series – the annual baseball championship series

LEARN MORE

Books

Gitlin, Marty. *St. Louis Cardinals (Inside MLB)*. Minneapolis, MN: Abdo, 2011.

Kelley, K. C. *St. Louis Cardinals (Favorite Baseball Teams)*. North Mankato, MN: Child's World, 2014.

Web Sites

Baseball History
http://mlb.mlb.com/mlb/history/
Learn more about the history of baseball.

MLB.com
http://mlb.com
See pictures and track your favorite baseball player's stats.

St. Louis Cardinals—Official Site
http://stlouis.cardinals.mlb.com
Watch video clips and read stories about the St. Louis Cardinals.

INDEX